songs of blue acorns

monoku

peter jastermsky

ISBN: 978-81-19654-99-4

First Edition: 2024
Rs. 200/-

Cyberwit.net
HIG 45 Kaushambi Kunj, Kalindipuram
Allahabad - 211011 (U.P.) India
http://www.cyberwit.net
Tel: +(91) 9415091004
E-mail: info@cyberwit.net

Printed at Repro India Limited.

When you want to know how things really work, study them when they're coming apart.

- William Gibson

great unknowns

choice making then the mice arrive

where the arrow falls subtract one

the forest or the trees

in the neck of time

math from the underworld let them count crows

prone to confabulating a hornet's nest in her fingertips

a mind body problem ants don’t connect

word traveler not my typo

hell withholds an *o*

nursing no illusions posthuman widget

hushed atmospherics the irony of air quotes

mind reading the tightlipped ventriloquist

great unknowns famous for not explaining

if you say so songs of blue acorns

dare to infer

life sentence rereading the escape clause

thinking it over thinking

shots in the dark second guessing the light switch

deep in asteroid country no discount on air bags

interpreting her sideways glance revocable trust

dare to infer dripping peach

taking it all off strip mining

by the clearcut one assumes

pleasure vortex another button undone

big thirsty news swallows from the water table

attentional hygiene the value of slow pour overs

sloe gin tides a red eye egret

wrangling corpuscles i bite into something bloodless

performative exuberance a convocation of falutins

muckraking for truth the one safe mushroom

ever the grammarian she pauses for a coma

impossibly private

deep bruising hurts we call home

over a dying reef glass bottom boat selfies

smoke scented towels we wrap ourselves in barbecue

after the sirens coyote karaoke

doomsday prevention a run on fat-free whipped cream

lounging in crosshairs politics in all directions

annual coup overthrowing the sock drawer

anointed as normal the terrors of good taste

soft open mouths of rivers impossibly private

bombed-out buildings all the versions of me

throwback machine animating the bygones

god-shaped holes fill with litanies

in the dead eye of an atom one loathsome persona

shaking hands every doorknob licked

iterations and personas one more cancelled name

melting every pronoun samba wind

untying the knot

up all night the stars say *so what*

the sound of your name in a mattress shedding tears

worry stone scouring the shoreline for solace

smiles until she spells *gruesome*

untying the knot lives at loose ends

out of round his heart's one good wheel

unlucky pants a bad trip uncuffed

toppled cairn any memories will do

the light in me draws moths

hoodoos and dust devils we are never the same

salt in wound plotting the kill shot

bones out of mud a friendless condition

empath the last time I *feel* you

bone on bone god doesn't have forever

life review bullshit gets real

welfare check following the blow flies

poetry morgue a perfect forever home

ACKNOWLEDGEMENTS

My grateful thanks to the editors of the following publications in which present or earlier versions of some of these poems first appeared: Bones, Cold Moon Journal, dadakuku, Failed Haiku, haikuNetra, Half Moon Day, Heliosparrow, Kontinuum, LEAF, Modern Haiku, NOON: journal of the short poem, Presence, Prune Juice, Under the Basho, and Weird Laburnum.

www.ingramcontent.com/pod-product-compliance
Lightning Source LLC
LaVergne TN
LVHW010119170826
845678LV00012B/2491

* 9 7 8 8 1 1 9 6 5 4 9 9 4 *